Sports Illustrated KIDS

All-Star Sports Trivia

Fun Facts You Need to Know!

Library of Congress Cataloging-in-Publication Data
available upon request.
ISBN 978-1-62937-952-4

This book is available in quantity at special
discounts for your group or organization.

For further information, contact:
Triumph Books LLC
814 North Franklin Street
Chicago, Illinois 60610
(312) 337-0747
www.triumphbooks.com

Produced by Shoreline Publishing Group LLC
Santa Barbara, California
Designer: Tom Carling, Carling Design Inc.

Text and photo research
by James Buckley Jr.

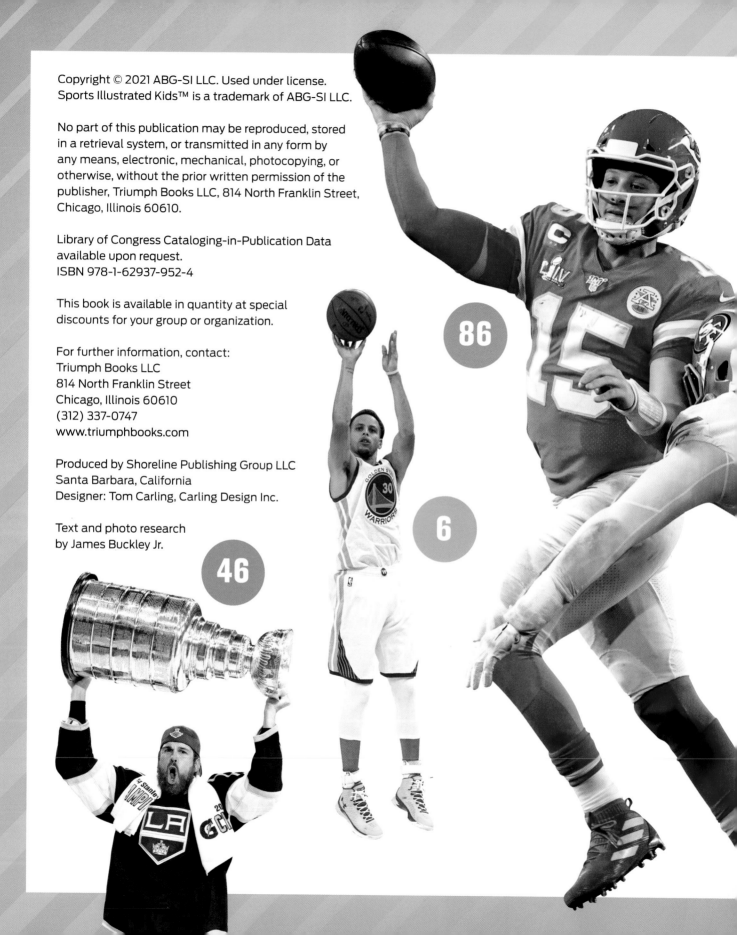

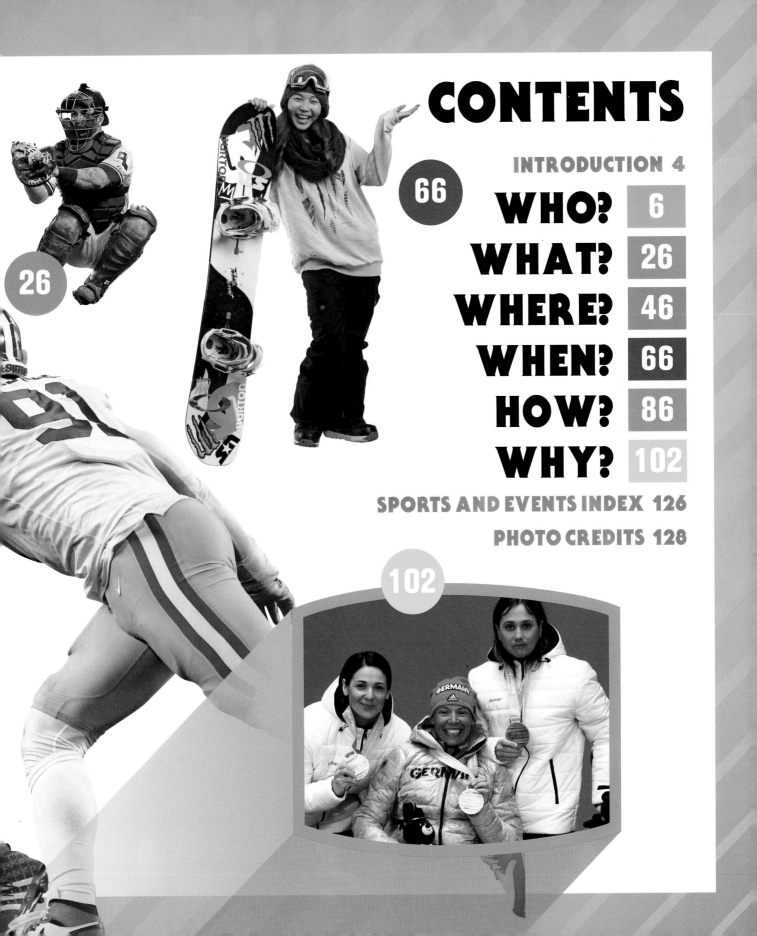

CONTENTS

WHAT?

DAYTONA

HOW?

WHY?

WHERE?

WHO?

WHEN?

INTRODUCTION

To a sports fan, there's nothing trivial about sports! We love everything about our favorite games and athletes. But some things are more well-known than others, and that's where "sports trivia" comes in. Sure, you know how many points a touchdown is or who LeBron James is or why Alex Morgan is famous. But take another step deeper into the sports world and you discover a ton of interesting stuff—how much do you know? That's what this book is about.

Using these famous six words, we'll ask (and answer) some questions about sports. You'll probably know some of the facts, but there will be some you don't—and you'll even learn more about the answers you *do* know.

Then, the fun part: Challenge your sports-loving friends and see how they do on your own trivia quiz. Who will win? What will they know? How will they celebrate? Game on!

WHO?

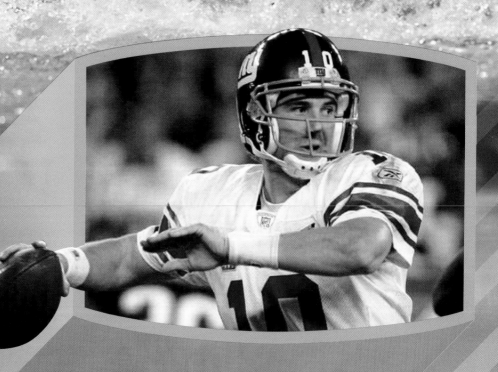

Who won? Who lost? Who was the first? Who scored the most? Without a whole lot of "whos," there wouldn't be any sports. The games we love are about the people who play them, who thrill us when they take the field, the court, the pool, or the gym. In this chapter, test your trivia skills about who did what in the world of sports.

★ ALL-STAR TRIVIA ★

Two other players have won the
award with two teams.
Kareem Abdul-Jabbar won with
the Bucks and the Lakers.
Kawhi Leonard was a Finals MVP
for the Spurs and Raptors.

Who was the first player to be named NBA Finals MVP with three different teams?

The King needs his bling! **LeBRON JAMES** earned the Bill Russell Award as the NBA Finals Most Valuable Player with the Miami Heat, Cleveland Cavaliers, and Los Angeles Lakers. James jumped right from high school to the NBA, drafted first overall in 2003 by his hometown Cleveland Cavaliers. He was the Rookie of the Year before starting a string of 17 straight NBA All-Star Game appearances in 2005.

He won a pair of regular-season MVP trophies with Cleveland, but didn't lead the Cavs to the NBA title . . . yet. He signed with the Heat for the 2010–11 season and won his first Finals MVP in 2012. Teamed with superstars Chris Bosh and Dwyane Wade, James won another championship ring and Finals MVP in 2013.

In 2014, he thrilled hoops fans in Ohio by returning to the Cavs. He put the team on his back and led them to the 2016 NBA Finals, where they set a record by bouncing back from being down three games to one to beat the Golden State Warriors. NBA Finals MVP for Team No. 2: Check!

Always looking for a new challenge, James signed with the Lakers before the 2018-19 season. In 2020, when the NBA moved into the "bubble" amid the COVID-19 crisis, James rose to the occasion. He led the Lakers to their 17th NBA title by beating the Heat. James proudly accepted the Finals MVP a fourth time. The King was in the house!

Who is the NFL's all-time touchdown leader?

In football, touchdowns are the ultimate reward for any single play. The NFL is more than 100 years old, and no one scored more TDs than **JERRY RICE**. Combining sure hands, speed, and incredible moves, Rice reached the end zone 208 times. That's 33 more than the player in second place on the all-time list, Emmitt Smith with 175.

In 1986, Rice's second NFL season with the San Francisco 49ers, he led the NFL with 15 TD receptions. He was tops in the league five more times in his 20-year career, including a then-record 22 scoring catches in 1987. In all, he had 197 TD catches; not surprisingly, that's also an NFL record. Rice ran for 10 more TDs. Wait, that's only 207. How did he get to 208? In the last game of the 1995 season, Rice flopped on top of a fumble by teammate Adam Walker in the end zone.

Who was baseball's first designated hitter?

Keeping pitchers out of the batting order has been discussed in baseball since the late 1800s. But it was not until 1973 that the DH was added—to the American League. The National League, then and now, voted against using it. On April 6, 1973, **RON BLOMBERG** of the New York Yankees stepped to the plate as the first DH in history. He walked with the bases loaded.

In 2020, to help pitchers' arms during the COVID-19, every team in Major League Baseball used a designated hitter for the first time. By 2021, it was back to business as usual, with the DH in use only in American League ballparks.

Who has won the most Gold Gloves for fielding excellence?

Fans and players appreciate great fielding in baseball. A player with a great glove and super throwing arm can help his team win game after game. The league honors the top fielders at each position in each league with the Rawlings Gold Glove Award. Pitcher **GREG MADDUX** won 18 Gold Gloves in his 23-year Hall of Fame career. Among non-pitchers, the great Baltimore Orioles third baseman Brooks Robinson is tops with 16 Gold Gloves.

When he wasn't fielding, Maddux was pretty good at pitching, too. He won four Cy Young Awards in a row from 1992–95, was a four-time NL ERA champ.

Who won the first WNBA MVP award?

It's hard to believe today, but when the WNBA was starting out in 1997, it couldn't find the address for a player who would become one of the league's all-time greats. **CYNTHIA COOPER** had been a two-time NCAA champ and a two-time Olympian. But when she called a WNBA team asking how she could join the new league, they said they'd been looking for her! Once that all got straightened out, Cooper-Dyke joined the Houston Comets and led them to the WNBA's first championship. She was named the league's first MVP in 1997, and won the award again in 1998. She also earned the first four WNBA Finals MVPs while leading her team to titles in 1997, 1998, 1999, and 2000.

Who is the WNBA's all-time leading scorer?

On June 18, 2017, **DIANA TAURASI** gave her dad a Father's Day present to remember. With a right-handed layup against the Los Angeles Sparks, she scored her 7,489th point, setting a new WNBA career mark. Her dad was among the thousands in the arena and millions of fans worldwide who cheered Taurasi's accomplishment. It was another in a long list of successes for the former University of Connecticut star. Since joining the Phoenix Mercury as the first overall pick of the 2004 draft, she has become a hoops legend. Taurasi is a 10-time all-star, a two-time WNBA Finals MVP, and has made the All-WNBA team an amazing 14 times. Still going strong at age 39 in the 2021 season, her all-time record points total continues to grow.

Who was the first Black tennis player to win the singles title at Wimbledon?

The Championships at Wimbledon in England began in 1877. The U.S. National Tennis Championships began in 1881 (it was not called the U.S. Open until 1968). But it was not until **ALTHEA GIBSON** came along that a Black player took part in those two important events. Already a champ in the all-Black American Tennis Association, Gibson played at the U.S. championships for the first time in 1950 and at Wimbledon in 1951. In 1957, Gibson won Wimbledon. Later that year, she won the U.S. National Championship, in both cases establishing firsts that probably should have come a lot earlier in history. Gibson ended her career with 11 Grand Slam titles in singles and doubles.

Who was the first woman to be an NFL game official?

A longtime college football official, down judge **SARAH THOMAS** first blew her whistle on an NFL field in 2015. Thomas grew up playing softball and basketball in Alabama, and began working as an official at grade school football games. By 2006, she was officiating college games before getting the call from the NFL. In 2021, she made history again as the first woman to work a Super Bowl as an official.

Who is the all-time leader in goals in international soccer?

I n a 2020 game against St. Kitts and Nevis, Canada's **CHRISTINE SINCLAIR** banged in a goal. That gave her a career total of 185 in her 290 international games, the most by any player, male or female. She topped the record set by American Abby Wambach. Sinclair started piling up goals when she earned a spot on the national team in 2000, when she was just 16. She was part of five World Cup teams for Canada, too. In 12 seasons in pro soccer, she also has 90 more goals (through July 2020)!

Who invented the Paralympics?

World War II left many members of the military with spinal injuries. In England, **DR. LUDWIG GUTTMANN** was treating some of them. He believed that sports and exercise would help them recover. In 1948, he started the Stoke Mandeville Games, named for a hospital. Only 16 athletes took part, but it started a movement. By 1960, the Games had expanded and became the Paralympics, held for the first time in Rome. Today, Summer and Winter Paralympics are held for athletes with spinal injuries and vision issues. In 2021, more than 500 athletes took part in 24 sports as part of the Tokyo Paralympics.

Who was the Big O?

Y ou've got to be pretty special to own a letter of the alphabet. But in the sports world, there is only one "Big O," basketball Hall of Famer **OSCAR ROBERTSON**. A 12-time NBA All-Star, NBA MVP, and three-time NCAA scoring champ, he was one of history's great all-around players.

Robertson grew up in Indiana, where he led his high school team to two state championships. At the University of Cincinnati, he led the NCAA in scoring three times and led the Bearcats to a pair of Final Four appearances. In 1960, he led the U.S. Olympic team to the gold medal at the games in Rome. After being drafted first overall by the Cincinnati Royals in 1960, he was named NBA Rookie of the Year for the 1960–61 season and earned the first of 12 straight All-Star Game selections. In his second season, he averaged double figures in points (30.8), assists (11.4), and rebounds (12.5). It was the first time any player averaged a triple-double for a season. He also had 181 career triple-double games — a record not broken until 2021! Robertson won his only NBA title in 1971 with the Milwaukee Bucks.

The Big O was a great all-around player, able to put up high scoring totals while also dishing assists and crashing the boards. His ability to do it all inspired generations of players to excel at all parts of the game.

★ ALL-STAR TRIVIA ★

With four consecutive victories in one event — the 200-meter butterfly—Phelps matched Carl Lewis as the only Americans with such a streak. Lewis won the long jump in 1984, 1988, 1992, and 1996.

Who has more Olympic gold medals than any other athlete?

When **MICHAEL PHELPS** touched the wall first in the 200-meter butterfly race at the 2016 Summer Olympics, he broke a record that had been set more than 2,000 years earlier. The victory gave Phelps 13 career individual gold medals. That snapped a tie with the ancient Greek athlete Leonidas of Rhodes, who had piled up 12 victories in the ancient Olympic Games. Leonidas's final wins came in 152 BCE.

That is not the only Olympic medal record Phelps holds. With 28 overall medals, he has more than any other athlete. His record haul consists of 23 golds, 3 silvers, and 2 bronzes. The 23 golds are also a record, and include 10 golds in relay events. It might be another 2,000 years before anyone tops his 13 individual golds.

Born in Baltimore, Maryland, Phelps made his first Olympic appearance when he was only 15, but he didn't earn a medal at those Games in Sydney, Australia. Four years later, he made his first big Olympic splash with six golds in Athens, Greece, in 2004. He then competed in the Olympics of 2008, 2012, and 2016. The big highlight was the 2008 Games, when he broke Mark Spitz's record by winning eight gold medals at a single Olympics.

Being that good for that long is rare in the sport of swimming. In fact, that 200-meter butterfly win also made Phelps, at 36 years old, the oldest individual swimming gold medalist since the great Duke Kahanomoku in 1920.

Who set the NBA record for most three-point baskets in postseason history?

The Golden State Warriors' sharpshooting guard, **STEPHEN CURRY**, holds just about every important three-point shooting record. He is the only player with four seasons of more than 300 treys; his 402 three-pointers in 2015–16 is the all-time single-season record. He leads the way with 536 games with at least three three-pointers. He is also first all-time in games with four, five, six, seven, eight, nine, ten, eleven . . . and twelve baskets from outside the arc.

The Warriors depend most on Curry in the playoffs, and, not surprisingly, he has come through big time. Through the 2020–21 season, Curry had poured in 470 three-pointers in 112 postseason games, by far the most ever. Along the way, he helped Golden State win three NBA championships.

Stephen's father, Dell, was also a top NBA shooter, and his brother, Seth, has been in the NBA since 2013. But Curry's shooting skill is more than great genes. Few players work harder and longer on their shooting than he does. His pregame shooting practice is so famous that fans head to the arena early to watch; it's sometimes even broadcast live. Until they move the arc farther from the basket, Curry figures to keep adding to his record — then again, not even that might stop him.

Who won the 2019 Vezina Trophy?

The NHL honors players and people from the past by putting names on all of its major awards. One of the most well-known is the Vezina Trophy for the NHL's top goalie. NHL general managers vote on the award, and after the 2018-19 season, **ANDREI VASILEVSKIY** of the Tampa Bay Lightning was named that season's winner. It was the first Vezina Trophy for the Russian native. He led the NHL in wins for a goalie with 31 and posted the best goals-against average of his career at 2.21. Since 2017–18, he has been in the top three in voting for the Vezina every year.

This award was named for Montreal Canadiens goalie Georges Vezina. One of the top netminders in the early days of ice hockey, he played from 1910 to 1925. He helped the Canadiens win the Stanley Cup in 1916 and 1924, and recorded the NHL's first shutout. He died of tuberculosis in 1926 at the age of 39. In his memory, the first Vezina Trophy was awarded to Montreal's George Hainsworth after the 1926–27 season.

Who is men's golf's all-time leader in major tournament titles?

Golf for men has four "major" tournaments. Together, they are known as the Grand Slam. The oldest of the four majors is the British Open, which was first played way back in 1860. In all the many years since, the top name on the Grand Slam leader board is **JACK NICKLAUS**. His 18 major tournament championships are three more than Tiger Woods, who is second.

Known as "The Golden Bear," Nicklaus burst onto the golf scene with his first PGA Tour victory at the U.S. Open in 1962. In each of the next 17 seasons, he won at least two PGA Tour events. He won both the Masters and the PGA Championship for the first time in 1963. He completed the career Grand Slam with a win at the British Open in 1966. Major tournament title No. 18 came in dramatic fashion in 1986. At the age of 46, he earned his record sixth Masters green jacket. Long retired, he remains an important force in golf as one of the world's most well-known golf course designers.

Who is the all-time leader in major golf tournament titles among women?

While the Grand Slam events for men's golf have remained the same since the Masters began back in 1934, the list of majors for women has changed over time. The U.S. Women's Open began in 1946, while the Women's PGA Championship started in 1955. Three majors began more recently: the Women's British Open (1979), the ANA Inspiration (1983), and the Evian Championship (2013). Other events such as the Titleholders Championship, the Western Open, and Nabisco Dinah Shore were considered majors for a while.

One golfer piled up the most wins in all of the women's majors: **PATTY BERG**. Before World War II, she was a national champion amateur before serving three years in the U.S. Marines during the war. Berg played in some pro tournaments — and won eight majors — in the late 1940s, and became a driving force behind the creation of the LPGA in 1950. By the time she retired in 1962, she had won an all-time record 15 major championships. That total included the first U.S. Women's Open 1946.

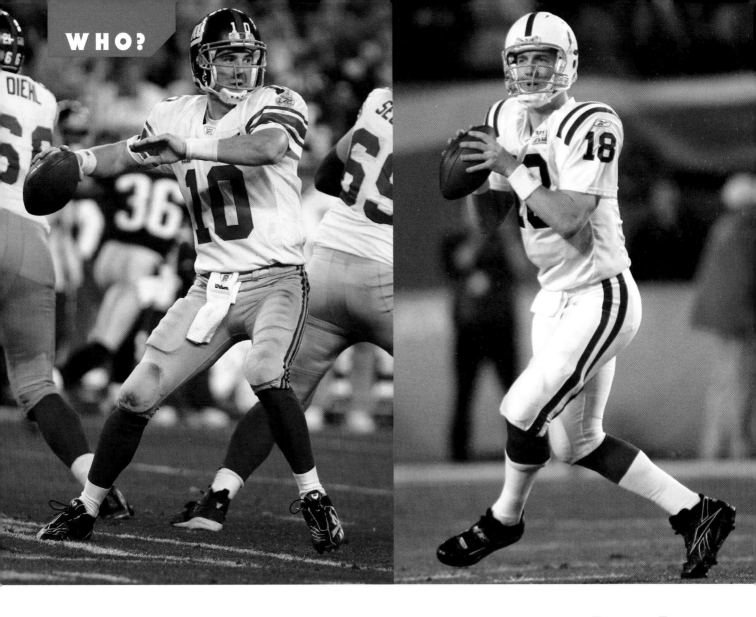

Who are the only brothers to both win Super Bowl MVP trophies?

Having one Super Bowl MVP in a family is pretty good — but only one family can claim a pair. Following in the cleats of their NFL quarterback father, Archie Manning, both **PEYTON AND ELI MANNING** led their teams to Super Bowl championships while also bringing home the Pete Rozelle Award as the Super Bowl MVP.

In his 10th season, Peyton led the Indianapolis Colts to Super Bowl XLI against the Chicago Bears. He was solid as usual, throwing for 247 yards on 25 completions. The longest was a 53-yard touchdown strike to Reggie Wayne. After holding up the Lombardi Trophy, he took home the MVP award for his performance.

Brother Eli made it two Mannings in a row in Super Bowl XLII. Eli's New York Giants faced off against the undefeated New England Patriots and Tom Brady. In one of the NFL's biggest upsets, Eli led New York to a 17–14 victory. The big play was his long throw downfield that David Tyree caught by clutching the ball to his helmet!

Who was the first woman to win four national championships in drag racing?

Drag racing has offered many opportunities for women to be part of the top ranks of motor sports. **ERICA ENDERS** has taken full advantage. In 2020, she became the first woman to win a quartet of titles in the challenging Pro Stock division. She's also now the all-time leader among female drivers in national championships, topping the record of three held by Shirley Muldowney (Top Fuel) and Angelle Sampey (Pro Stock Motorcycle). Enders started drag racing when she was eight years old, and was a pro when she was a teenager. Pro Stock cars that (sort of) look like regular production vehicles.

★ ALL-STAR TRIVIA ★

Shirley "Cha Cha" Muldowney was the first woman to win a national championship in drag racing. In her hot-pink dragster, she captured the Top Fuel title in 1977, then repeated the feat in 1980 and 1982.

WHAT?

Asking "what?" covers a lot of ground. The answer might be an award, a game, a record, a nickname, a bit of sports slang, or much more. We narrowed it down to a few things you might be wondering about. See how much you can show about what you know!

What is the name of the award given each year to the top pitchers in baseball's American and National Leagues?

When you win way more games than any other pitcher, an award gets named for you. Since 1956, the top pitchers in Major League Baseball have taken home the coveted **CY YOUNG AWARD**. Young won an all-time record 511 games in his 22-year Hall of Fame career from 1890 to 1911. How far ahead is he? In second place is Walter Johnson, with a measly 417 wins! Young might have actually earned the Cy Young Award in several seasons—if they had voted on it back then. He led his league in wins five times, with a high of 36 in 1892. He was a two-time ERA champ as well. And though no one had heard of WHIP yet, he posted the best numbers in that stat in seven seasons. Young also holds all-time records for losses, starts, and innings pitched. And he threw a perfect game in 1904.

When MLB created the award, at first it was given to just one pitcher, not to one in each league. Don Newcombe of the Brooklyn Dodgers won the first Cy Young Award. Sandy Koufax of the Los Angeles Dodgers won three in the 1960s. Beginning in 1967, a winner was named in both the AL and NL. Roger Clemens is the all-time leader with seven Cy Young Awards. He won three with the Boston Red Sox, two with the Toronto Blue Jays, one with the New York Yankees, and a final one with the Houston Astros at the age of 42 in 2004.

2020 AL Cy Young Award winner Shane Bieber of Cleveland

What is the "12th man" in football?

Football teams only get to have 11 players on the field for each play. So who is the 12th man? The answer is, well . . . **YOU, THE FAN**. Pro and college teams rely on the fans to cheer and encourage them. This loud and loyal support has led some teams to give the folks in the seats this nickname.

In college, the tradition started at Texas A&M. In a 1922 game, the Aggies were getting crushed by Centre College. They lost several players to injuries and the coach was getting desperate. A backup player named E. King Gill had been given the week off to help with other duties at the game. When called by the coach, he left his seat in the stands, suited up, and got ready to play. Inspired by Gill, his teammates came back to win the game. Though Gill didn't even get into the game, the school has used his example ever since to demonstrate the importance of the people in the stands.

In the NFL, the most famous 12th man group is in Seattle (above). Fans there are so loud that they once triggered an earthquake warning alarm. They repeatedly create trouble for opponents, making so much noise that signals can't be heard on the field. Before each game, the team raises a ceremonial No. 12 flag. In 1984, the number was retired so that no Seahawks player will ever wear it again.

What is Tiger Woods's real first name?

The most famous big cat in sports was not born Tiger Woods. His parents, Earl and Kutilda, named him **ELDRICK TONT WOODS** when he was born on Dec. 30, 1975. The origin of the name Eldrick is a mystery, but Tont means "beginning" in Thai, the native language of Woods's mom. Earl Woods soon began calling his son Tiger after a soldier he had served with in the Vietnam War. Col. Vuong Dang Phong was in the South Vietnamese army, fought alongside Earl Woods, and was nicknamed "Tiger." Sadly, Col. Vuong was killed in the fighting, but when Earl Woods had a son, he remembered his late friend. Eldrick became Tiger to one and all.

He has certainly lived up to his ferocious name, becoming one of the most successful athletes in the world. Tiger Woods has won 82 PGA Tour events (tied for most ever), and has 15 Grand Slam wins, second most all-time. He is far and away the all-time money-winner with more than $120 million in prize money. His long-drive power changed the sport, and his fist-pumping victory celebrations created many new fans.

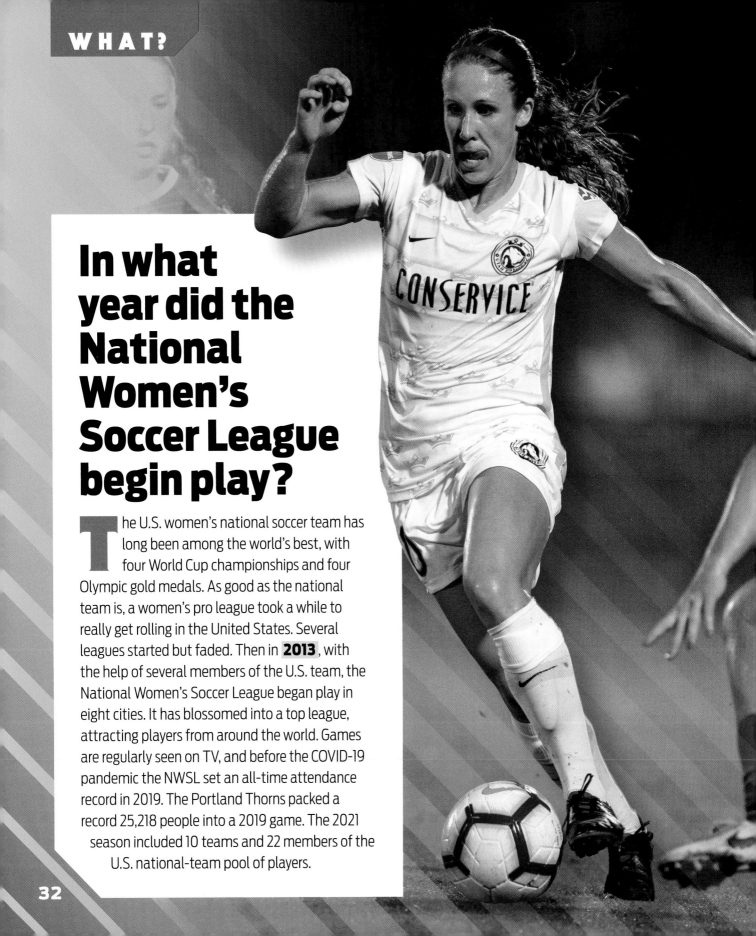

In what year did the National Women's Soccer League begin play?

The U.S. women's national soccer team has long been among the world's best, with four World Cup championships and four Olympic gold medals. As good as the national team is, a women's pro league took a while to really get rolling in the United States. Several leagues started but faded. Then in **2013**, with the help of several members of the U.S. team, the National Women's Soccer League began play in eight cities. It has blossomed into a top league, attracting players from around the world. Games are regularly seen on TV, and before the COVID-19 pandemic the NWSL set an all-time attendance record in 2019. The Portland Thorns packed a record 25,218 people into a 2019 game. The 2021 season included 10 teams and 22 members of the U.S. national-team pool of players.

What is the most famous NASCAR race?

Most sports feature their biggest event at the end of a long season. NASCAR does things a little differently. The first full-field race of each year is the **DAYTONA 500**, by far the most famous race on the annual schedule. The first stock car racing in Daytona actually came not on a track, but on the hard-packed sand of the Florida beach. As the popularity of the races grew, local promoter Bill France Sr. built a 2.5-mile oval racetrack. On Feb. 22, 1959, at the brand new Daytona International Speedway, 59 cars started in the first Daytona 500. As would be the case at many future events, the ending was thrilling. Lee Petty and Johnny Beauchamp battled on the final straightaway and flashed under the checkered flag at nearly the same instant. It took three days to find the photos that showed that Petty had just barely won. From then on, the legend of the famous race grew and grew. Lee Petty's son, Richard, holds the record with seven Daytona 500 victories, followed by Cale Yarborough with four.

What is the biggest tournament played by European pro soccer clubs?

The best soccer teams in Europe have two big goals every season. The first is to win their national league, whether that is in England, Italy, Spain, Germany, or any of the other 51 countries that are members of the Union of European Football Associations (UEFA). European soccer, however, offers another competition that has become the second-biggest tournament in the world, after the World Cup. The champions in each league earn a spot in the **UEFA CHAMPIONS LEAGUE**. The top leagues also earn spots for teams that finish second, third, or fourth. The summertime Champions League draws fans from around the world to see the top teams and best players battle for the trophy.

The event began in 1955 and was first called the European Cup. Beginning in 1992, it became the Champions League. Through 2021, Spain's Real Madrid has won the most titles with 13. Italy's AC Milan is second with seven. In 2021, Chelsea of the English Premier League emerged as the champion.

Mason Mount of Chelsea (Premier League) celebrates with the 2021 Champions League trophy.

French rider Sylvain Chavenel powers through a mountain stage in the Tour de France.

What is the world's most important cycling race?

How does a long bicycle ride through beautiful countryside scenery sound? Pretty nice, right? Well, the **TOUR DE FRANCE** is all that, but at top speed, through tightly packed crowds, and for more than a month and 2,000 miles. Leave this ride to the pros!

Since 1903, the Tour has been the biggest race on the annual road cycling calendar. Today's cyclists push up mountain roads and through winding streets on high-tech bikes, sometimes reaching speeds of up to 60 miles per hour. Riders win points for their finish each day, with more points given if they win a daily stage. The leader each day gets to wear the famous yellow jersey. In recent years, the Tour has expanded outside France to include stages in Belgium, Germany, Italy, and the Netherlands. The finish line, though, remains in Paris. Jacques Anquetil, Eddy Merckx, Bernard Hinault, and Miguel Indurain are tied for the most overall victories with five.

What is the record for most Women's World Cup titles?

The United States women's soccer team got the Women's World Cup off to a great start, winning the first one in 1991. (The men's World Cup has been around since 1930, so what took so long to start the Women's, right?) Michelle Akers scored a pair of goals as the U.S. beat Norway 2–1. Eight years later, the U.S. women got their second trophy when Brandi Chastain banged in a penalty kick after the U.S. and China tied in regulation play. The U.S. earned title number three with a huge 5–2 win over that same nation in 2015. Carli Lloyd scored a hat trick in just 15 minutes, including a majestic goal from midfield! The U.S. added to its record total with a fourth World Cup title in 2019. Megan Rapinoe and Rose Lavelle each scored to set off the celebration. The 2023 Women's World Cup will be played in Australia and New Zealand.

Megan Rapinoe leads the U.S. celebration after the 2019 Women's World Cup.

What sport uses terms like "wicket," "googly," and "silly mid-off"?

The answer is **CRICKET** — the sport, not the insect. This bat-and-ball game has been a huge part of British culture since it became popular in the 1700s. As the British Empire spread around the world, it took the sport with them. Today, cricket is enormously popular in India, Pakistan, Australia, South Africa, and other places once ruled by Great Britain. The annual Cricket World Cup is watched by more than 1 billion people around the world. As for those unusual words? The wicket is what the bowler is aiming at, sort of like home plate in baseball. A googly is a nickname for a ball that twists and curves on the way to the batter. And the silly mid-off is a fielding position.

The batsman gets set to protect the wicket from the bowler's googly!

In hockey, what is a "lamplighter"?

At NHL games, when **A GOAL** is scored, a goal judge pushes a button that activates a bright red light behind the goal. That lets everyone in the arena know that a goal has been scored (seeing that tiny puck from high up in the arena can be tricky!). A lamplighter is a player who makes that light go on a lot. Wayne Gretzky was the ultimate lamplighter. The Hall of Fame center scored an NHL-record 894 goals in 20 seasons. Among NHL players still active, Washington's Alex Ovechkin leads the way with 730 career "lamplightings" through the 2020–21 season.

What was the first year girls were allowed to play Little League Baseball?

Little League Baseball is the world's biggest youth baseball organization. It began in **1939** in Williamsport, Pennsylvania. Girls, however, were not allowed to play officially until 1974. It took a ruling by a court to force Little League to make things fair for all players. Hundreds of girls signed up, and Little League started a softball league to give even more girls a chance to play. Today, more than 2 million kids play in the organization around the world. Through 2019, 19 girls had played in the Little League World Series. The most famous of those was pitcher Mo'Ne Davis, who starred for her team in 2014.

Mo'Ne Davis

What makes the Boston Celtics home court unique?

The wooden floors of NBA courts are often decorated with wild designs, interesting colors, and of course, all the lines needed for play. One court remains unique, however. The Boston Celtics home court is made up of 264 squares, each made of pieces of lumber that form a checkerboard pattern called **PARQUET** (par-KAY). The team first played in the Boston Garden in 1946. That was just after World War II and long pieces of lumber were hard to find. So workers gathered thousands of smaller pieces. Workers assembled the many pieces into the parquet pattern. It became a symbol of the Garden and team. The Celtics brought the floor with them when they moved to the TD Garden in 1995.

Julian Edelman and Tom Brady celebrate after the New England Patriots won Super Bowl LIII.

What NFL team won the most games in the 2000s?

The **NEW ENGLAND PATRIOTS** started play in 1960 as the Boston Patriots of the old American Football League. They joined the NFL in 1970. Over the next 30 years, they had some pretty good seasons, twice reaching the Super Bowl, only to lose. But they were never really a dominant force.

That changed in 2000 when Bill Belichick took over as head coach, and a year later when Tom Brady became the team's starting quarterback. For the next 20 seasons, the Patriots enjoyed a run of success almost unmatched in NFL history. They won 244 games in those years — 27 more than the runner-up Pittsburgh Steelers. New England won at least 10 games each year from 2003 through 2019. In the same span, they won the AFC East Division every season but one (they were second in 2008, when Brady missed 15 games with an injury). In the 2000s, they also an incredible nine AFC Championships.

The Pats won their first Super Bowl in the 2001 season and repeated the feat five more times. Their record-tying sixth Super Bowl win (matching the Steelers) came with a 13–3 win over the Los Angeles Rams in Super Bowl LIII.

Through it all, Brady and Belichick led the way. The dynasty ended when Brady left to join the Tampa Bay Buccaneers for the 2020 season — of course, he led them to a Super Bowl championship, too! Belichick and the Pats will have to start all over again.

What school has won the most women's college basketball championships?

Few schools have been so good for so long as the University of **CONNECTICUT** women's hoops teams. The Huskies won their first national championship in 1995, led by star Rebecca Lobo and coach Geno Auriemma. The coach is still on the job 25 years later, and he has led his team to 10 more national titles. That's one more than UCLA, the men's all-time title champ.

UConn won three in a row from 2002 through 2004, with a lot of help from superstar Diana Taurasi. The Huskies went back-to-back in 2009 and 2010 led by Maya Moore (right). And the 2013 to 2016 teams did even better, winning four straight.

The Huskies own the longest winning streak by any college basketball team, men or women, at 111 games (2014 to 2017). Guess who has the second-longest streak? That's right, the Huskies, with 90 more consecutive Ws (2008 to 2010). That second streak included a pair of undefeated seasons that ended with national titles. Their most recent title came in 2016 with a huge win over Syracuse. Current WNBA star Breanna Stewart led the Huskies to that record-setting 11th national championship.

In what alpine skiing series did Lindsey Vonn win more races than any other woman?

Alpine skiing is the name for the high-speed races such as downhill, slalom, and giant slalom. Since 1967, the world's top alpine skiers have competed in the **WORLD CUP**, a series of events held on mountains around the world (but mostly in Europe). At each event, skiers can take part in seven types of races. It takes great skill, versatility, and stamina to win week after week, and that makes the feats of American superstar Lindsey Vonn that much more impressive. She retired in 2019 with 82 World Cup race wins, the most ever by a woman and second most all-time to Ingemar Stenmark's 86. Vonn also won four overall World Cup Championships, awarded to the skier who piles up the most points in a full season of races.

What are the "tools of ignorance"?

Playing catcher in baseball is one of the toughest jobs in sports. You get hit by foul balls, bats, and pitches. Baserunners can crash into you. And you have to crouch down for most of a three-hour game. Catchers do wear **PROTECTIVE GEAR**, but it's still a hard gig. Muddy Ruel played in the Major Leagues from 1915 to 1934, and he came up with this nickname for the mask and pads that catchers wear. Why ignorance? He meant that if you put these on, you probably didn't know what you getting yourself into.

What is the blue line in hockey?

Two blue lines are painted in the ice for a hockey game. Each line is about a third of the way from the goal line and marks the beginning of a **TEAM'S DEFENSIVE ZONE**. The blue line is important because it marks the place where offsides can be called. An offensive player cannot go past the blue line before the puck has crossed it. Getting into the zone without being offsides takes split-second timing; a linesman waits at each blue line to call the penalty or wave his arms to show that offensive players can proceed.

What is a "dime" in basketball?

A dime is an **ASSIST**. A player earns an assist when her pass leads directly to a basket. For example, if Player A dribbles into the lane and then passes to Player B, who then drops in a layup, Player A gets an assist. Guards are usually the key assist makers, but every player is expected to help out by passing to an open teammate. In 2020, Courtney Vandersloot of the Chicago Sky (left) set the WNBA single-season assist record with 9.95 per game. Longtime Utah Jazz star John Stockton set the NBA mark in 1989–90 when he averaged 14.5 per game.

In a stadium . . . on a rink . . . inside an arena . . . around a racetrack . . . on a golf course, a basketball court, and more — every sport takes place somewhere. Combine a little geography, a little history, and your knowledge of the world of sports, and see how well you do in knowing where the answers are to all these questions!

WHERE?

Where is the Green Monster?

The Green Monster is the nickname of the left-field wall in **FENWAY PARK**, home of the Boston Red Sox since 1912. That year, the ballpark was squeezed into the Fenway neighborhood in the capital of Massachusetts. Team owner John Taylor thought too many people could stand behind a regular height left-field wall and get a free peek at the action. So Taylor had a tall wooden wall built there. The wall stood 25 feet high along Landsdowne Street. For very popular games, fans were sometimes allowed to sit inside the wall (for a fee!) on a small mound of dirt.

In 1933, however, a fire destroyed most of the ballpark. When Fenway Park was rebuilt, the wall returned, and at 37 feet tall it was bigger than ever. A 23-foot net was added to the top to keep baseballs from flying into traffic outside. Large advertisements covered most of the Monster until 1947, when it was first painted its famous Fenway Green color. The scoreboard in the base of the wall is still operated by people sitting inside the wall during games. In 2003, the net came down and the Red Sox added about 250 Monster Seats in rows atop the wall. The Green Monster remains one of the most familiar stadium landmarks in sports.

Where is the penalty spot in soccer?

The penalty spot is not where penalties occur — otherwise, players would just avoid it! Instead, players attempt penalty kicks from the spot, which is located **12 YARDS FROM THE CENTER OF EACH GOAL LINE**. Teams are awarded penalty kicks when a serious foul is called inside the penalty area, the 18-yard-deep box in front of and to the side of the goal itself. No defense except the goalie is allowed, and the goalie can't move forward until the ball is kicked.

Not surprisingly, most penalty kick attempts go in. It's a short shot and the goalie is often helpless to stop it. However, that puts the pressure on the shooter, and there are many legendary stars who have booted this easy kick over the net or to the side. Goalies who make miraculous stops can become national heroes.

In major tournaments, games that remain tied after overtime are decided by a penalty-kick shootout. Each team gets five penalty kicks; whoever makes more is the winner.

Where is the key in basketball?

Basketball's key doesn't open up anything, but it is the key area of the game. The key is a rectangle of **SPACE UNDER AND IN FRONT OF EACH BASKET**. Most courts outline the key, also known as the lane, in colored paint. In the NBA, the key is 16 feet wide and ends at the free-throw line, 15 feet from the basket. In high school and college basketball, the key is four feet narrower.

Offensive players cannot stay in the key for more than three seconds in a row. In other words, no camping under the basket waiting for rebounds.

But why is it called a key? Shouldn't it be the "box"? The answer is in basketball history. Until 1951, the rectangle in front of the basket was only six feet wide. The circle at the top of the key, surrounding the free-throw line, was still a circle. Put those two shapes together and they formed (sort of) a key shape (see photo). Actually, it looked more like a keyhole, but that didn't work as a nickname.

★ ALL-STAR TRIVIA ★

Until 2008, international basketball's key was shaped like a trapezoid. It was wider at its base than at the free-throw line.

Where is the Frozen Tundra?

The non-sports answer is that all tundra is frozen tundra. Tundra is land in the Arctic region that is so cold that it freezes year-round. In sports, though, the Frozen Tundra is a nickname given to **LAMBEAU FIELD** in Green Bay, Wisconsin, home of the Packers since 1957. Green Bay can get very, very cold in the winter — but the games go on. In 1967, the Packers played the Dallas Cowboys in the NFL Championship Game. The temperature was -13ºF, and the grass turf was frozen and icy. When NFL Films made a movie about the game, writer Steve Sabol said the game was played on the "frozen tundra" of Lambeau Field. Since then, the nickname has become synonymous with the stadium and the magic of the Packers. However, the turf there can't freeze anymore. Today, pipes with flowing warm water are buried under the grass to prevent freezing.

Where is college baseball's World Series played each year?

Unlike the World Series in Major League Baseball, which is played at the ballparks of the two competing teams, the College World Series has a permanent home. Since 1950, the tournament that decides the NCAA baseball champion has been played in **OMAHA, NEBRASKA**. Until 2013, it was played at that city's Rosenblatt Stadium. The event is now played at the new TD Ameritrade Arena. Eight teams make the final tournament, split into two groups of four. They play double-elimination games, with the group winners meeting in the championship. Unlike the MLB World Series, the CWS is best-of-three.

USC has won the most CWS tournaments, with 12 wins. Its most recent was 1998. Louisiana State and Texas are tied for second with six each. More than two dozen players have won both a CWS and a World Series, with Roger "The Rocket" Clemens (Texas and the Yankees) perhaps the most well-known.

Where did all these NFL stars play college football: Don Hutson, Joe Namath, Ken Stabler, Derrick Henry, and Tua Tagovailoa?

I n 2020, the **UNIVERSITY OF ALABAMA** had 56 players on NFL rosters, the most for any college or university. The Crimson Tide was also tops in 2018 and 2019. It's not surprising to see so many Alabama players make the NFL, given that the school has had a lengthy run of success. They have won or shared six national championships since 2009, capped by a victory in the 2020 College Football Playoff title game.

Hutson was the NFL's first superstar receiver. With the Packers in the 1930s and 1940s, he set many NFL records. Namath and Stabler were Super Bowl–winning quarterbacks for the Jets and Raiders, respectively. Henry was a Heisman Trophy winner and later an NFL rushing champ. And QB Tagovailoa (above) leads the Miami Dolphins after being chosen in the first round of the 2020 NFL draft.

Where does a tight end line up in football?

Combining pass-catching skills with the ability to block for teammates, the tight end has become a key part of the offense on most NFL teams. The tight end usually lines up right **NEXT TO THE TACKLE** on one side of the offensive line. Early football teams often did not have this position. Players who could catch passes were all lined up farther out from the ends of the line, or in the backfield. As new offensive plays came to the game in the 1940s, the idea of having a player handle two roles — blocking and receiving — caught on.

In the 1960s, Mike Ditka and John Mackey became stars as tight ends, mostly for their pass-catching. By the 1980s, players like Kellen Winslow were leading teams in catches and touchdowns. Tony Gonzalez, Rob Gronkowski (right), and Travis Kelce have set all-time tight end records for catches, yards, and touchdowns. Gonzalez's 1,325 career catches are the most by a tight end. Gronk's 17 TD catches in 2011 set a single-season record for tight ends. Kelce has the receiving yards mark with 1,416 in 2020.

Where did American star Hilary Knight play pro ice hockey?

A two-time NCAA champion at the University of Wisconsin, Knight is one of the best players ever. The Idaho native joined the U.S. national team in 2006 as well and has brought home a room full of medals. Knight starred on Olympic silver-medal-winning teams in 2010 and 2014. In 2018, she led the U.S. team to its first gold since 1998. She played pro hockey in **BOSTON AND MONTREAL**. As of 2021, she had become one of the leaders of the Professional Women's Hockey Players Association, which hopes to re-start a pro league in the United States and Canada soon.

Where do the Kings, Clippers, Lakers, and Sparks play?

The **STAPLES CENTER** in downtown Los Angeles is a very busy place. In 2021, four major pro sports teams all made their homes there. The Kings play in the NHL, the Sparks in the WNBA, and the Lakers and Clippers in the NBA. That might change in 2024 when the Los Angeles Clippers are scheduled to move to their own arena to the south in Inglewood. The Staples Center is filled with sports action more than 200 days a year. That's not to mention concerts that are squeezed in when there are no games scheduled. With the NBA and NHL seasons happening at about the same time, the switch back and forth between an ice hockey rink and a basketball court has to happen fast. During the NBA and NHL playoffs, games from each sport might be held on the same day. Staples Center workers can remove the wooden basketball court to reveal and prepare the ice to get set for hockey in only a few hours.

Where did softball superstar Jennie Finch play in college?

Few athletes have dominated a sport like the great softball pitcher Jennie Finch. She was the pitcher on national champion age-group teams at 12, 14, and 18. In high school, she won 50 games, threw six perfect games, and had a tiny ERA at 0.15. From 2000, she led the **UNIVERSITY OF ARIZONA** Wildcats to three College World Series appearances, including the 2003 title. That season, Finch earned her second first-team All-America spot, and was named the MVP of the WCWS and national player of the year. In 2001-02, she set a record with 60 wins in a row!

Finch also helped the United States Olympic team win the gold medal in Athens, Greece, in 2004, as well as a silver in 2008. Her career record with the national team, including World Championships and Pan American Games, is 38–2. The hard-throwing righthander also starred for the Chicago Bandits of the National Pro Fastpitch League, going 35–8 until her retirement in 2010.

Where is the Brickyard?

That is the famous nickname for the **INDIANAPOLIS MOTOR SPEEDWAY**. When the famous speed palace opened in 1909, the track itself was actually made of bricks laid down on top of sand and dirt. It made for a rough ride in the early days, but gave the place its famous nickname.

Over time, the bricks were removed or covered with asphalt. However, a ceremonial strip remains at the start/finish line. Winners of the NASCAR Brickyard 400 and the Indy 500 always kiss the bricks in honor of the racetrack's long tradition.

Jules Rimet Trophy awarded at 1930 World Cup.

Where was the first soccer World Cup played?

A few years before the 1932 Olympics in Los Angeles, soccer was dropped as one of the Olympic sports. When FIFA, the world soccer organizing body, heard this, they planned their own tournament as a replacement. The first World Cup was played in **URUGUAY** in the summer of 1930. Uruguay's team was the most recent Olympic champion. Also, an economic depression had hit Europe hard and many cities were struggling. That was not the case in Montevideo, Uruguay's capital. Thirteen teams headed to the event, including a team from the United States. The tournament began on July 13. On July 30, home team Uruguay scored the final three goals of the championship match to come from behind and win the Cup 4–2.

Where is the Wimbledon tennis tournament played?

The answer is right there in the question: Wimbledon, England. That's the name of a suburb of London where the event is played at the **ALL-ENGLAND LAWN TENNIS AND CROQUET CLUB**. However, the sneaky part of this question is that the tournament is not officially called "Wimbledon." The best men's and women's players are actually playing in The Championships. Still, fans and players alike refer to the event simply as Wimbledon.

The tournament is the only Grand Slam event held on grass courts. It was first was held in 1877, and the event is packed with tradition. Players are not allowed to wear any color clothing except white. And strawberries and cream is the traditional snack between matches.

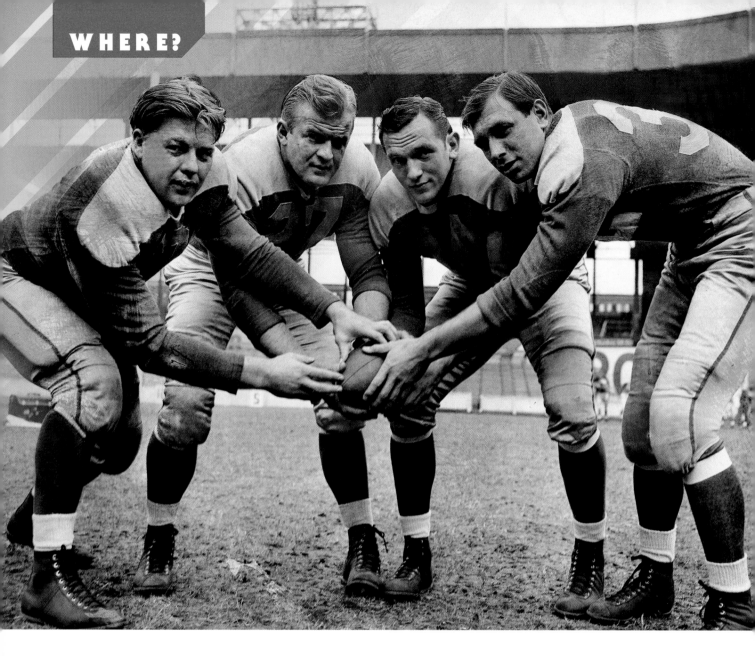

Where did the NFL's Rams first play?

Few NFL teams have moved around as much as the Rams. They started play in 1937 in **CLEVELAND, OHIO.** In 1945, the Cleveland Rams won the franchise's first NFL championship. A year later, the Rams moved to Los Angeles to become the first NFL team on the West Coast. In 1979, the team moved to Angels Stadium in Anaheim, south of Los Angeles — but they were still called the L.A. Rams. In 1994, they packed up again, this time moving east to become the St. Louis Rams. The 1999 Rams won the franchise's only Super Bowl (so far!), led by strong-armed quarterback Kurt Warner.

In 2016, the team moved . . . again! This time it was back to California, where they played in the downtown Los Angeles Coliseum. In 2020, the team moved into SoFi Stadium in Carson, a suburb of L.A. It looks they're here to stay — although with this history, the Rams might want to keep a few bags packed!

Where was Angels star Mike Trout born?

MILLVILLE, NEW JERSEY, leaped onto the sports map when hometown hero Mike Trout started bashing baseballs all over the major leagues. Trout grew up in the small town, about 45 miles east of Philadelphia, and was a high school star there. He was drafted by Los Angeles in the first round of the 2009 draft. By 2012, he was in the majors, where he was named the AL Rookie of the Year. In Trout's first eight seasons, he won three MVPs and finished second in the voting four other times. He is considered one of the best overall players in the game today; he combines power, speed, batting average, and defense better than anyone else. In OPS, which measures power and ability to get on base, he is tops among active players at more than 1.000. For all his success, Trout remains humble and loyal. He and his family still live in Millville in the offseason.

Where did the great Michael Jordan play college basketball?

The **UNIVERSITY OF NORTH CAROLINA** has produced a few dozen of the best basketball players of all time, along the way winning seven NCAA championships and 18 Atlantic Coast Conference tournament titles. But one of those players rises above the rest — the great Michael Jordan. MJ first played with the Tar Heels in the 1981-82 season. He buried the game-winning basket to clinch North Carolina's 1982 National Championship win over Georgetown. As a sophomore and junior, he led the team in scoring, was named an All–American, and won national player of the year honors.

He was the third pick in the 1984 NBA draft by the Chicago Bulls. He led them to their first NBA Championship in 1991 and then helped them add five more. Jordan also won five MVP awards, six NBA Finals MVP trophies, and 10 scoring titles. He was dominant at both ends of the court, and is considered by many the greatest all-around player in NBA history. And it all started when he wore Carolina blue.

Where were the 1984 Summer Olympic Games held?

In 1984, **LOS ANGELES** became the first American city to host the Summer Olympics for a second time. L.A. had also been home to the 1932 Games. The Los Angeles Coliseum, a stadium built for those '32 Games, was also the main home of the '84 Games. More than 6,700 athletes from 140 countries came to Southern California. Fans from around the world filled stadiums, arenas, fields, and tracks to watch more than 20 sports. The only blemish was the absence of any teams from the Soviet Union. They had boycotted the Games to protest the American team boycotting the 1980 Olympic Games in Moscow because of the USSR's invasion of Afghanistan. Nevertheless, the L.A. Olympics provided some incredible memories for American athletes. Carl Lewis won four gold medals in track and field. American women won 11 gold medals in swimming, while Mary Lou Retton won the all-around gold in gymnastics.

WHEN?

Whether the game was last night, last week, or last year ... it happened sometime! Sports fans always keep a sharp eye on the calendar and the clock so they know when their favorite teams and athletes will be playing. Once the games are over, everyone remembers when their best sports memories happened. See how well you can do on this chapter of trivia about when things occurred in sports.

When did Wayne Gretzky first set the single-season NHL scoring record?

H e was known simply as "The Great One." Few athletes have had as big an impact on their sport as Wayne Gretzky did on the National Hockey League. In **1980-81**, his second NHL season, he scored 164 points to top the old record of 155. A year later, he topped himself — Gretzky scored an incredible 92 goals and had 120 assists, giving him a points total of 212 that no one, not even Gretzky, topped since (through 2021). His 92 goals in a single season also set a record that still stands.

Gretzky did more than set records, of course. He led the Edmonton Oilers to four Stanley Cup titles, earning a pair of Conn Smythe Trophies as playoffs MVP. As for those records, Gretzky's only competition was himself, so in 1985–86, he set a new single-season mark with 215 points. No player has come within 16 points since then. In fact, Gretzky still owns nine of the top 11 point-scoring seasons in NHL history, and had 13 seasons with 130 or more points.

Gretzky won an incredible nine NHL MVP Awards and later led the Los Angeles Kings to their first Stanley Cup Final appearance. He also played with the St. Louis Blues and New York Rangers. After he retired in 1999, he became a hockey executive with teams in Phoenix and Edmonton, while also helping to direct Canada's national hockey team. In 2000, the NHL retired his No. 99 jersey for all teams in the league. "The Great One" is the only hockey player to receive that honor.

When did Monday Night Football begin?

It might not seem like a big deal now, but when ABC Sports' Monday Night Football was first shown on **SEPTEMBER 21, 1970**, it was revolutionary. Until that night, just about every NFL game ever had been played on a Sunday. Saturdays were reserved for college football. But NFL officials were looking for something new, and, led by NFL Commissioner Pete Rozelle, they convinced ABC to show a Monday game. Thanks to the national popularity of the sport, and also partly to the very interesting announcer Howard Cosell, Monday Night Football was a huge hit right from the start. Since then, the NFL has also played regular-season games on Thursdays and Saturdays.

> Through 2020, the Miami Dolphins had played in the most MNF games, with 76. The most recent in 2019 featured QB Ryan Fitzpatrick.

When did baseball's World Series begin?

The World Series played these days between the American and National League is actually the second "World's Series." From 1884 to 1890 (and again in 1892), the NL champ played a team from the American Association. However, Major League Baseball recognizes the **1903** World Series as the first of the modern age. The Boston Americans (later the Red Sox) beat the Pittsburgh Pirates five games to three that year. The next year, the NL-champion New York Giants refused to play Boston, again the AL champs. By 1905, however, the World Series was officially an annual part of the sports calendar. It has been played every year except 1994, when a players' strike ended the season early and cancelled the event.

WAGNER, PITTSBURG

When did Ichiro Suzuki get his 3,000th career hit?

On **AUGUST 7, 2016**, Ichiro Suzuki of the Miami Marlins smacked a triple to right field for the 3,000th hit of his amazing Major League career. He became the first player from Japan to reach that milestone. A big reason for his achievement was his MLB-record 10 straight seasons with 200 or more hits, including an all-time single-season record of 262 hits in 2004. In 2001, he had also been named both the Rookie of the Year and AL MVP with Seattle. Suzuki retired in 2019 after 3,089 hits, ten All-Star selections, and 10 Gold Gloves.

When did an American woman most recently win the LPGA Player of the Year Award?

Men's pro golf includes some champions from outside the United States, but for the most part, the top male players are American. That's not the case with women's pro golf. The sport has long featured great players from around the world. In recent years, South Korea has sent a lot of top players to the LPGA.

The last American woman to be named the Player of the Year was **STACY LEWIS**, in 2014. Before her, Beth Daniel had won way back in 1994. To win the award, Lewis led the LPGA in winnings at more than $2.5 million, and won three tournaments. She also had more top-10 finishes than any other golfer. Before Lewis, Sweden's Annika Sorenstam won the award eight times. Since Lewis's 2014 win, golfers from South Korea and Thailand have taken home the trophy.

When did the X Games begin?

The annual action-sports extravaganza began as the Extreme Games in **1995**. Among the sports in that first event in Rhode Island were skysurfing and bungee jumping! The big show became the X Games the next year and has since delivered thrills aplenty. The first Winter X Games was in 1997. Today, the X Games remain the top action-sports showcase, even as skateboarding and snowboarding have become Olympic sports as well. Male and female X Games athletes come from around the world to show off their skating, biking, snowboarding, skiing, and sometimes driving talents in search of gold medals.

When did the U.S. women's soccer team win their first World Cup?

Today, the U.S. women's national soccer team is the best in the world, winners of four World Cups, more than any other nation, and consistently ranked as the world's best. It all started with the first Women's World Cup in **1991**, played in China. Twelve nations qualified for the event. The United States team dominated its opening group, winning three straight games and outscoring opponents 11–2. The U.S. won the first knockout game, a 7–0 rout over Taiwan, before smacking Germany 5–2 in the semifinal. The team was powered by its forward line. Twenty of the Americans' 25 goals were scored by just three players: Michelle Akers (right), Carin Jennings, and April Heinrichs. Jennings had a hat trick in the Germany game, while Akers piled up five in the Taiwan win.

In the first-ever Women's World Cup championship game, Akers scored twice. Her second goal gave the U.S. a 2–1 win over Norway. Jennings won the Golden Ball as top player, while Akers scored 10 goals to earn the Golden Boot as top scorer.

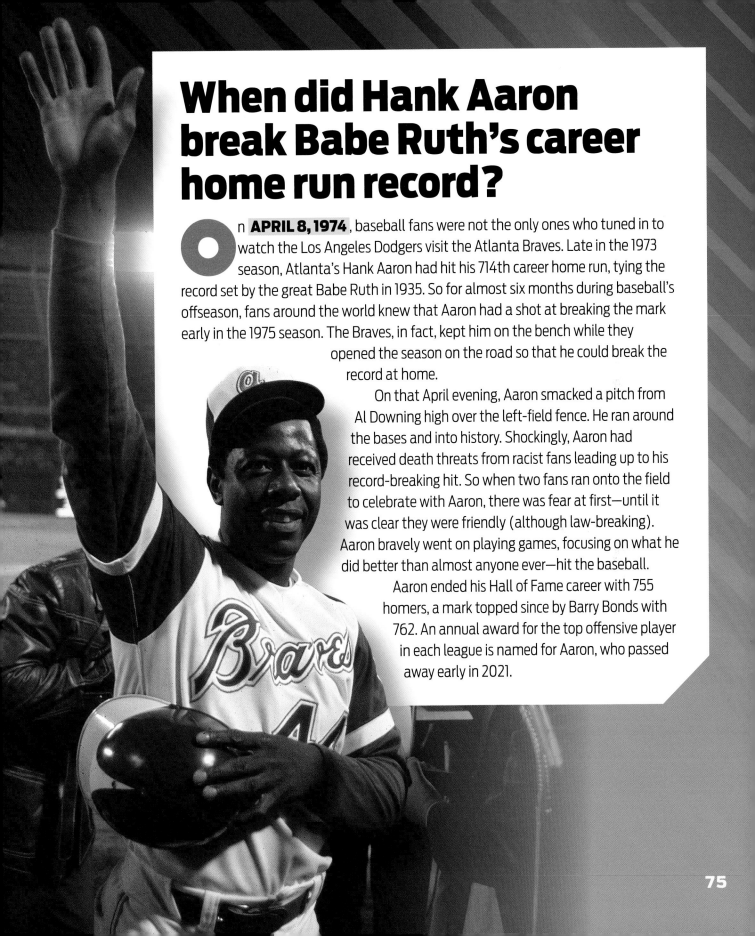

When did Hank Aaron break Babe Ruth's career home run record?

On **APRIL 8, 1974**, baseball fans were not the only ones who tuned in to watch the Los Angeles Dodgers visit the Atlanta Braves. Late in the 1973 season, Atlanta's Hank Aaron had hit his 714th career home run, tying the record set by the great Babe Ruth in 1935. So for almost six months during baseball's offseason, fans around the world knew that Aaron had a shot at breaking the mark early in the 1975 season. The Braves, in fact, kept him on the bench while they opened the season on the road so that he could break the record at home.

On that April evening, Aaron smacked a pitch from Al Downing high over the left-field fence. He ran around the bases and into history. Shockingly, Aaron had received death threats from racist fans leading up to his record-breaking hit. So when two fans ran onto the field to celebrate with Aaron, there was fear at first—until it was clear they were friendly (although law-breaking). Aaron bravely went on playing games, focusing on what he did better than almost anyone ever—hit the baseball.

Aaron ended his Hall of Fame career with 755 homers, a mark topped since by Barry Bonds with 762. An annual award for the top offensive player in each league is named for Aaron, who passed away early in 2021.

When did Chloe Kim win her first X Games gold medal?

At the **2015 WINTER X GAMES**, Chloe Kim did a face-plant on an early superpipe run. But a few minutes later, she put aside her pain and worry and shredded her final run. When the scores were announced, she had become the youngest person ever to earn a gold medal at the Winter X Games. "My face kind of hurts right now, but that was so fun," she said afterward. She was only 14 years old!

It was just the start of a great snowboarding career. In the years since, Kim has earned an Olympic gold medal, plus six more X Games medals through 2021, including three golds. She is the two-time world champion in halfpipe and has won eight World Cup events as well.

When did the Arizona Diamondbacks and Tampa Bay Rays join Major League Baseball?

Major League Baseball had grown to 28 teams in 1993 . . . but team owners thought there was room for more. Since they had to add two at once to keep the leagues balanced, MLB voted to award new teams to ownership groups from Tampa, Florida, and Phoenix, Arizona. The Tampa group wanted to include fans from nearby St. Petersburg in the name, plus use a popular local sea animal as the mascot. So the Tampa Bay Devil Rays were born, and started play in **1998**. The team dropped the "Devil" part before 2007. The Rays are still seeking their first World Series title, but they did win the AL championship in 2008 and 2020.

Arizona joined the National League, also in 1998. The team name comes from a familiar local snake. Led by ace pitchers Randy Johnson (above) and Curt Schilling, Arizona won the World Series in 2001, only its fourth season. That topped the mark of the Florida (now Miami) Marlins, who began in 1993 and won the World Series in 1997.

When did an American skater first win the women's World Figure Skating Title?

The first World Figure Skating Championship for women was held way back in 1906. (The men had started 10 years earlier.) Skaters from Europe dominated, with Norway's Sonja Henie the big star. She won an amazing 10 straight titles from 1927 to 1936.

In **1953**, however, Tenley Albright (above) broke through as the first American world champion. At age 16, she had recovered from polio to earn a silver medal at the 1952 Olympics. She won again in 1955 at the world championships in Switzerland, and won the first Olympic gold for an American woman skater in 1956. She had a chance to become a pro, touring in ice shows to make money, but chose to return to school. She became a surgeon and medical school teacher!

When did Serena Williams become tennis's all-time leader in Grand Slams in the Open Era?

As she piled up Grand Slam title after Grand Slam title, the only question became when Serena Williams would top the Open Era record of 22, set by Steffi Graf. (Margaret Court Smith won 24 Grand Slams, but most came before 1968, when the Open Era began.) Williams's record-setter finally came at the **2017 AUSTRALIAN OPEN**. When she beat her older sister, Venus, in the final, she was overcome with emotion. It was Serena's 23rd Grand Slam singles title — including seven in Australia — and the most for any player, male or female, since tennis switched to all professionals. Williams's road to the top started in Compton, California, on courts that were often cracked or even missing nets. Serena won her first Grand Slam at the 1999 U.S. Open, and just kept going and going.

When did Clemson beat Nebraska to win the school's first college football title?

T he Clemson Tigers have been one of college football's best teams in the past decade. Led by stars such as Deshaun Watson, Travis Etienne, and Trevor Lawrence, Clemson has played for the national title four times since 2015. They won it all in 2016 and 2018. But that did not include the school's first title. Clemson started playing football in 1896, but didn't reach the top of the national rankings until the **1981** season. That year, they headed into a final game showdown with Nebraska in the Orange Bowl, with a probable national title on the line. Clemson had not been ranked before the season, but had climbed the polls with win after win. They were 11–0 entering the Orange Bowl. A TD catch by Perry Tuttle (above) was a key second-half score for Clemson. The final score was 22–15.

When did LaDainian Tomlinson set an NFL record with 186 points in one season?

The NFL record for points in a single season had stood for 46 years when the **2006** season began. Back in 1960, Green Bay running back Paul Hornung had scored 15 touchdowns. Hornung was also the team's kicker, so he got 41 more points on kicks after touchdowns and 45 points on field goals. His 176 total points remained the most until LaDainian "L.T." Tomlinson ran it right out of the record book.

L.T. had scored 18 touchdowns in 2005, and his 17 rushing TDs led the NFL the year before that. But he sprinted past those totals by Week 9 of the 2006 season, including a pair of four-TD games. With the first of two TDs he scored in a game against the Kansas City Chiefs in Week 14, Tomlinson broke Hornung's record. He ended the season with 186 points on 31 touchdowns; his 28 rushing TDs were also a single-season record. Tomlinson retired in 2011 with 145 rushing TDs, second most all-time behind Emmitt Smith of the Dallas Cowboys.

When did Simone Biles set a record with her 24th World Gymnastics Championship medal?

The chalk dust flew as Simone Biles stuck another perfect landing. It was the balance beam event at the **2019 WORLD GYMNASTICS CHAMPIONSHIPS** , and her 15.066 points gave her the gold medal. That result also gave her the world record for medals in world championships, with 24. That topped a record held by Russian male gymnast Vitaly Scherbo and cemented Biles's place as probably the greatest all-around gymnast ever.

She began piling up medals with a pair of golds at the 2013 world event—one in the all-around and another as part of the U.S. team. She won four each at the 2014, 2015, and 2018 World Championships. She topped herself in 2019 with five golds. Add in three silvers and three bronzes and you reach her final total of 25.

Her world championship medals also do not include the four golds and a bronze she won at the 2016 Summer Olympics and a silver and bronze at the Olympics in 2021!

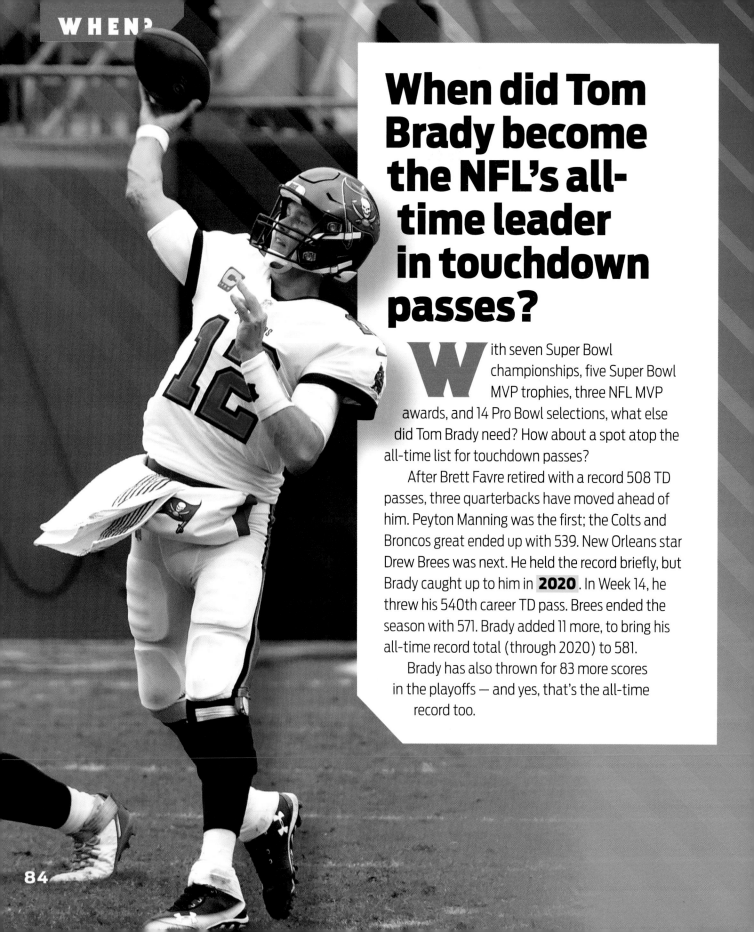

When did Tom Brady become the NFL's all-time leader in touchdown passes?

With seven Super Bowl championships, five Super Bowl MVP trophies, three NFL MVP awards, and 14 Pro Bowl selections, what else did Tom Brady need? How about a spot atop the all-time list for touchdown passes?

After Brett Favre retired with a record 508 TD passes, three quarterbacks have moved ahead of him. Peyton Manning was the first; the Colts and Broncos great ended up with 539. New Orleans star Drew Brees was next. He held the record briefly, but Brady caught up to him in **2020**. In Week 14, he threw his 540th career TD pass. Brees ended the season with 571. Brady added 11 more, to bring his all-time record total (through 2020) to 581.

Brady has also thrown for 83 more scores in the playoffs — and yes, that's the all-time record too.

When did the Seattle Storm win their first WNBA championship?

The Seattle Storm stormed to their fourth WNBA championship in 2020. Led by MVP Breanna Stewart's powerful scoring and Sue Bird's pinpoint passing, Seattle became the third WNBA team to make it to four titles.

The team's first championship came back in **2004**. Bird was in just her third season, and teamed with sharpshooting Lauren Jackson. Seattle finished second in the regular season behind the L.A. Sparks, but powered through two playoff rounds to reach the WNBA Finals against the Connecticut Sun. Seattle lost the first game, but bounced back in Games 2 and 3. Betty Lennox was named the Finals MVP after averaging 22.5 points per game.

Seattle went on to win three more championships in 2010, 2018, and, of course, 2020.

HOW?

ow much? How many? How often? How long? The questions just keep piling up, but we just keep coming up with the answers. "How" can also help discover the process of something, so watch for questions in this chapter about how something came to be part of the sports world. Now ... see how you do!

How did Babe Didrikson Zaharias make history?

What if gymnastics superstar Simone Biles was also a U.S. Open golf champion? Or if top golfer Michelle Wie was also a record-setting sprinter (as well as a national champion basketball player)? One woman actually did all those things: Babe Didrikson Zaharias. She was perhaps the **BEST ALL-AROUND FEMALE ATHLETE** in history. Babe Didrikson grew up in Texas, where the first sport she was great in was basketball. She got a job after high school with an insurance company, but she was really hired to play for its basketball team. She led them to a national championship in 1931. She also won a national title in track and field.

In 1932, she caught the attention of the world by winning a pair of gold medals at the Olympics in Los Angeles. She set a world record while winning the 80-meter hurdles. Her Olympic record in the javelin also earned her a gold medal. Babe added a silver in the high jump.

After the Olympics, she switched to yet another sport: golf. In 1938, she was the first woman to compete in a men's pro tournament. (That year, she married wrestler George Zaharias, too.) By the 1940s, she was one of the top female golfers and eventually won 10 major titles, including three U.S. Women's Opens. Babe passed away from cancer at age 45, but her legend remains. In 2000, *Sports Illustrated* chose her as the second-greatest female athlete of the 20th century, trailing only pentathlon star Jackie Joyner-Kersee. ESPN put Babe at number 10 overall; she was the first woman on their list after nine men.

How did the San Francisco 49ers get their name?

The numerical nickname for Californians from the Bay Area was born more than 70 years before the NFL! **IN 1849, GOLD WAS DISCOVERED** near Sacramento, California. Soon, tens of thousands of people poured into San Francisco on their way to the gold fields. These prospectors were nicknamed Forty-Niners. San Francisco itself grew from a small port to a huge city. California was just a territory of the United States at the time, but so many people came that in 1850 it became the 31st state. So when a new NFL team was created to join the league in 1946, the nickname was right there, ready for use. Fans of the Niners, as the team is often called, have watched some pretty golden teams. San Francisco is tied for second all-time with five Super Bowl titles.

How does putting chalk on their hands help gymnasts?

Performing gymnastics is hard work, and athletes can get sweaty. That can make it hard to grip some of the equipment they use, such as the uneven parallel bars and the pommel horses. The soft, powdery chalk they put on their hands **HELPS ABSORB SWEAT** so the gymnast will be less likely to slip off the equipment. Some gymnasts even put chalk on their legs to help on events like the high bar or parallel bars.

How do NHL players earn the Lady Byng Trophy?

The NHL is the only sport that gives out a trophy honoring a player's "**SPORTSMANSHIP AND GENTLEMANLY CONDUCT**." The award is named for Lady Marie Evelyn Byng, who created the award in 1925, when she was the wife of Canada's governor-general. Hockey can be a rough and hard-hitting sport, and players can pile up penalty minutes easily. A top player who doesn't take a lot of penalties and plays the game hard but fairly gets the most points for the Lady Byng from hockey writers, who choose the winner.

Frank Boucher of the New York Rangers won the most Lady Byngs, with seven through 1935. The great Wayne Gretzky won five to add to his huge haul of trophies. The 2021 winner was defenseman Jaccob Slavin of the Carolina Hurricanes, who was called for just a single penalty all season.

LeBron James celebrates with his Bill Russell Award in 2020. It was the fourth time James was named NBA Finals MVP.

How does an NBA player take home the Bill Russell Award?

The trophy honoring the **NBA FINALS MOST VALUABLE PLAYER** was named in 2009 for Bill Russell, the longtime Boston Celtics superstar. Russell played for the Celtics from 1956 to 1969 and was part of an incredible 11 NBA championships. He was the dominating star center for most of those years. In 1966, he became the first Black head coach in the NBA when he was named the player-coach; of course, he led his team to three more titles. Considered perhaps the best rebounder (he led the NBA five times in that department and is second all-time with 22.45 per game) and one of the greatest defensive players ever, Russell was elected to the Basketball Hall of Fame as a player in 1975 and as a coach in 2021.

How much does the winner of the Wimbledon tennis championship take home?

In 2006, Roger Federer won the Wimbledon tennis tournament singles title and $1.28 million in prize money. Aurelio Mauresmo was the women's champ; she got only $1.21 million. Venus Williams (above) had had enough. Before the 2007 tournament, she said she would not play until the prize money for men and women was the same. It was not a new idea. The U.S. Open tennis tournament started giving its male and female champions the same prize back in 1973. But Wimbledon was a holdout. Williams's strong stand forced the Wimbledon organizers to change the rules; since then, the male and female winners have been awarded the same prize money. Williams ended up winning in 2007, the fourth of her five Wimbledon championships. In 2021, the singles winners each received **$3.3 MILLION**.

How much does an American Olympic gold medalist earn?

Winning a gold medal is usually the peak of an athlete's career. It has taken years of hard work, effort, and sacrifice to reach their goal. The Olympics do not award prize money. Starting in 1994, the U.S. Olympic Committee joined dozens of other nations by finally providing cash awards. For the 2021 Summer Games in Tokyo, **U.S. GOLD MEDALISTS EACH GOT $37,500. PARALYMPIANS EARN $7,500 FOR GOLD MEDALS**.

How long is a basketball game?

NBA game clocks run for **48 MINUTES**, divided into four quarters of 12 minutes each. Of course, the actual game takes longer than that because of timeouts, fouls, halftime, and other stoppages. Figure to spend an average of 130 minutes watching an NBA game on TV or in person. The longest NBA game ever came way back in 1951, when Rochester and Indianapolis needed six overtimes before Indy won 75–73.

WNBA games are 40 minutes long, with two halves of 20 minutes each. That's the same as in NCAA men's play, while NCAA women's games are divided into four quarters of 10 minutes each. In 2001, Washington and Seattle made fans stay through a record four overtime periods before Washington won the longest WNBA game ever.

★ ALL-STAR TRIVIA ★

The NBA added the 24-second shot clock in 1954. Before that, teams could hold the ball for as long as they wanted. That made some games just seem like the longest ever!

How often are the Winter Olympics held?

Since the Winter Olympics began in 1924, the event has been held **EVERY FOUR YEARS**, just like the Summer Games. In fact, the Summer and Winter Games used to be held in the same calendar year. After the 1992 cycle, the International Olympic Committee decided to separate the Games, having either a Winter or Summer Olympics on the schedule once every two years. To put this new arrangement into place, a pair of Winter Games (1992 and 1994) were just two years apart. The 2020 Tokyo Summer Olympics were postponed to 2021 because of COVID-19 . . . but were still called the 2020 Games.

How many people does the NFL's largest stadium hold?

There are actually two answers to this question. The official capacity champion (that is, how many actual seats are there) is **METLIFE STADIUM** (pictured), home of both the New York Giants and New York Jets, with 82,500 seats. (It's also the answer to another trivia question: What stadium is in a different state than the city names of its teams? MetLife is in East Rutherford, New Jersey, across the Hudson River from New York City.) However, the single-game American record for largest attendance at an NFL game was set in 2009 at **AT&T STADIUM**, home of the Dallas Cowboys. Including more than 30,000 people who watched from standing-room only areas, a record-setting 105,121 fans were at that game.

★ ALL-STAR TRIVIA ★

The smallest NFL stadium is Soldier Field in Chicago. It can hold more than 61,000 people, though, so that's still pretty big!

How many women have raced in the Indy 500?

The Indy 500 is one of the most famous car races in the world. It began way back in 1911, but it was not until 1977 that a woman driver was on the starting grid. That year, Janet Guthrie became the Indy female pioneer. A blown engine knocked her out after 27 laps, but she returned the next year to finish ninth, and raced again in 1978. Since Guthrie, eight other women have taken part in the Indy 500. Sarah Fisher has raced the most among that group, with nine races. Perhaps the most famous female Indy driver is Danica Patrick (above). She took part in eight races, starting in 2005. She has the highest finish of any woman driver in the event; Patrick was third in 2009, and she briefly led the race, too.

How did Patrick Mahomes learn to throw a football so well?

Patrick Mahomes has taken the NFL by storm since joining the Kansas City Chiefs in 2017. In 2018, his first full season as the team's starting quarterback, he led the league with 50 touchdown passes, the youngest player ever to reach that mark (which, trivia fans, is second all-time to Peyton Manning's 55 in 2013). Mahomes has the ability to throw accurately from almost any angle or position. He has completed passes while falling forward and falling backward, and has even tossed some underhanded or lefthanded throws. He has also become an expert at throwing passes one way while looking another!

Mahomes certainly worked hard to perfect his passing power, but **HE CAN ALSO GIVE HIS FATHER A LOT OF CREDIT**. Patrick Mahomes, Sr., was a pitcher in Major League Baseball for 11 seasons. He began working with his talented son when Patrick Jr. was less than 10 years old. They used a lot of long toss, which is a baseball drill that like playing catch in which players move farther and farther away from each other. "My dad has had me long tossing since, well, forever," said the Chiefs QB. "I think that helped build arm strength, helped build accuracy and touch." With steady practice, some good genes, and a little help from dad, Patrick Mahomes is an NFL superstar.

WHY?

We started asking this question when we were just little sports fans, right? Why? It drove the parents crazy, but we just kept asking. In this chapter, the beat goes on as we look into why things happen in sports. The answers can be found in history, physics, barnyards, and the alphabet. Why? Why not!

Why are college football postseason games called bowl games?

After each college football season, fans eagerly look forward to the bowl games, postseason events seen as a reward for a great regular season. Over the years, games such as the Sugar Bowl, the Orange Bowl, and the Fiesta Bowl have become the settings for national championship games as well. The "Bowl" part in those names came **FROM THE FIRST ONE —THE ROSE BOWL**, a game that got its name from the actual stadium in Pasadena, Calif., where it was played.

Why "bowl," though? That name for a stadium was first used in New Haven, Connecticut, when the Yale Bowl opened in 1914. Its design looked like . . . a bowl. The Rose Bowl builders copied the name. A big game was played there in 1923, and the name of the stadium stuck to the name of the game.

Why do golfers line up their putts?

Putting greens are not flat. They have hills and bumps and curves. Golfers need to choose where to hit their putts to take all that into account. The best way is to stand behind the ball, crouch down, and **EYEBALL THE PATH THE BALL MIGHT TAKE**. The golfer visualizes how the ball will roll and change direction and how fast she needs to hit it. Like everything else, it takes practice to learn this key golfing skill.

Why are hockey pucks kept frozen?

A warm puck bounces, while a frozen one slides. Hockey pucks are made of vulcanized rubber. **TO PREVENT THEM FROM BOUNCING** too much and being harder to control, the NHL and other hockey leagues keep the pucks in a rinkside freezer. Officials can replace the puck when it warms up during play. In 2019, the NHL introduced pucks printed with a league logo that changes color to help refs look for warm pucks. When the NHL logo is purple, the puck is frozen.

Why does a basketball have a bumpy surface?

F riction is the physical force that slows down movement. In the case of a basketball, the bumps on the leather surface of the ball increase friction between a player's hands and the leather surface. Those bumps **CREATE MULTIPLE POINTS OF FRICTION**, making it easy to grip the ball. If a basketball was smooth, it would be very hard to grip and would easily slip out of a player's hands. It also might not bounce cleanly against the smooth floor.

Andrea Eskau of Germany happily shows off her gold medal for the 10-K biathlon at the 2018 Paralympic Winter Games.

Why do Olympic and Paralympic champions receive gold, silver, and bronze medals?

The first modern Olympic champions in 1896 didn't get a gold medal. They got a silver medal and a laurel wreath. Second-place finishers got bronze, and third-place got a handshake! In 1904, **PERHAPS TO SET THE FIRST AMERICAN-HOSTED GAMES APART**, at the St. Louis Olympics, the tradition of gold, silver, and bronze medals began. The tradition stuck, and new gold, silver, and bronze medals are made for each Games.

Why do baseball relief pitchers wait in the "bullpen"?

Bullpens were around long before baseball, of course. That's where actual bulls were kept on ranches and farms. Just how the word became part of baseball is a bit of a mystery, though. One theory is that some fans **IN THE 1800S WERE HELD BEHIND ROPES "LIKE CATTLE,"** so they said. The area was soon also used by pitchers warming up. Another idea comes from Bull Durham tobacco signs, which had a picture of a large bull, that were featured in many small ballparks in the 19th century. Pitchers warmed up behind some of the signs, leading to the bullpen name.

Why did a law called Title IX change women's sports?

In 1972, the United States passed a long list of new laws about education. One of them, numbered Title IX (that's nine in Roman numerals), said that schools had **TO CREATE EQUAL OPPORTUNITIES IN SPORTS** for both men and women. Up to that point, men's sports got all the money and attention; many schools did not even offer women's sports. The new law forced schools to give girls and women many new opportunities. Since then, hundreds of thousands of female athletes have been able to play sports, thanks to Title IX.

Why do swimmers flip when they turn at the end of each lap?

Flip turns **SAVE PRECIOUS TIME** in races where fractions of a second count. The flip turn was created in 1936 by American backstroker Adolph Kiefer and his coach Julian Robertson. In a flip turn, a swimmer gains momentum by diving under the water, flipping over, then pushing off the wall with his or her legs. Before the flip turn was created, freestyle and backstroke swimmers simply touched the wall with their hands at each end of the lap, then turned around and swam the other way. The flip turn is not used in the breaststroke or butterfly.

Swimmer Megan Wujciak shows how a flip turn is done.

111

Pittsburgh's Sidney Crosby plants the traditional winner's kiss on the Stanley Cup in 2017.

Why is the NHL's championship trophy called the Stanley Cup?

From 1888 to 1893, Lord Frederick Arthur Stanley was the governor general of Canada. That meant he was the representative of the Queen of England, who officially still ruled Canada. **LORD STANLEY** fell in love with the country's favorite sport, hockey. In 1889, he presented a silver bowl to hockey league organizers, to be awarded to the top team in Canada. His name quickly was linked to the Cup, which he wanted to call the Dominion Hockey Challenge Cup. Stanley is a better name, though, right?

Why do sports officials sometimes wear black and white stripes?

Referees in football, hockey, and basketball, among other sports, wear the shirts **TO STAND OUT FROM THE PLAYERS** on both teams. The classic look was created in 1920 by Lloyd Olds. He was the referee in a football game between Arizona and Michigan State. The white shirt he wore looked like an Arizona jersey and players were getting confused. Lloyd and a friend created the black-and-white striped shirt and started using it the next year in basketball games. The look caught on across sports.

Eyeblack in place, Notre Dame's Kurt Hinish waits to take the field.

Why do so many athletes wear eyeblack?

The theory is that the black stripes of grease or black-colored stickers **ABSORB LIGHT** that might otherwise bounce off cheekbones into the athletes' eyes. The first eyeblack was made with burnt cork rubbed under each eye. Sticky black grease came next, and today's athletes can choose premade stickers, sometimes with words or numbers printed on them. But does eyeblack work? Scientists are not sure, with some studies saying it makes no difference. However, to the athletes who use eyeblack, it has one undeniable thing going for it — it looks really cool.

Why is it called a turkey when you get three straight strikes in bowling?

Bowling three straight strikes used to be a lot harder than it is today. More than 100 years ago, on holidays such as Thanksgiving and Christmas, **OWNERS OF BOWLING ALLEYS WOULD GIVE A LIVE TURKEY AS A PRIZE** to the first person on each team who got three strikes in a row. The name stuck even when living fowl was not on the line during games.

Why was Red Grange called the "Galloping Ghost"?

Harold "Red" Grange was the first national superstar in football. He started his career at the University of Illinois, racing past and around opponents with blinding speed. In one game against Michigan in 1924, he scored four touchdowns in 12 minutes. Afterward, famous sportswriter Grantland Rice wrote that Grange was a "**GRAY GHOST** thrown into the game/that rival hands may never touch." From that, the nickname Galloping Ghost was born. Grange became a pro in 1925 and his huge popularity and great skill helped establish the young NFL in the hearts of sports fans.

Why was Dominique Wilkins called "The Human Highlight Reel"?

Just who gave the great NBA forward that memorable nickname is lost to the mists of time, but the reason for it was clear—few players made as many eye-catching and highlight-worthy plays. Wilkins first thrilled fans with his high-flying dunks in high school. Then he was the SEC Player of the Year at Georgia, and played the first 12 of his 16 NBA seasons with the Atlanta Hawks, beginning in 1982. **WILKINS SEEMED TO SOAR ABOVE OPPOENTS, FINISHING OFF SLAMS WITH FLAIR AND STYLE**. He won the NBA Slam Dunk Contest in 1985 and 1990, and finished second to Michael Jordan in 1988.

Why do golf balls have dimples?

As a golf ball soars away after being hit, air flows around it. The **DIMPLES CREATE WHAT IS CALLED A TURBULENT LAYER OF AIR ON THE SURFACE OF THE BALL**. That layer lets air flow farther around the ball, preventing some of the drag, or air resistance, that would slow the ball down. If a golf ball was smooth, it would only go about half as far.

Why are tennis balls yellow and fuzzy?

Tennis balls are fuzzy so they will **CREATE FRICTION** when they bounce. This slows the ball down and makes it easier to control. It also causes the ball to roll on a racket or the court surface instead of sliding. Players are better able to predict what the ball will do. A fuzzy ball also grabs the court more than a smooth one would.

Why are field hockey fields wetted down?

Most fields in top-level field hockey are made from artificial turf. Wetting the field with water before games helps **REDUCE THE FRICTION** between the ball and the turf. That means the balls don't bounce as high and move more consistently and smoothly when rolling on the ground. Also, the water makes the ground softer, protecting players who fall.

Why do motor sports race winners speed past a checkered flag?

Checkered flags tell drivers there are no more laps to be run. The winner "takes the checkered flag" by driving past it first. But why checkered? Auto historian Fred Egloff notes that in the early 1900s, car makers held rally races that were hundreds of miles long. Many cars broke down, however. So in 1906, Sidney Waldon, who worked for the Packard Motor Car Company, created the flag to signal where cars could stop to be repaired. A famous photo from that year shows race winners speeding past a large checkered flag. A tradition was born!

Why do many pro soccer clubs' names include "FC"?

While nearly all American sports teams are named with a location and a nickname, European soccer teams are run by sports clubs. In some cases, the people of a city or town run the club and sponsor the team. In Europe, soccer is called "football," so clubs got names such as Liverpool FC or FC Barcelona. **THE FC, OF COURSE, STANDS FOR "FOOTBALL CLUB."** In the United States, some Major League Soccer and National Women's Soccer League teams have followed the European example. Fans in the United States can cheer for teams such as FC Cincinnati (MLS) and FC Kansas City (NWSL).

Lindsey Horan stars for Portland Thorns FC of the NWSL.

Buffalo Bills quarterback Josh Allen

Why is the NFL team in Buffalo called the Bills?

The team's name originates not in upstate New York but on America's western plains. An earlier Buffalo pro team was called the Bills in honor of frontiersman and entertainer **BUFFALO BILL CODY** (left). Buffalo Bill's Wild West Show brought the excitement of the "Wild West" to audiences across America and Europe in the late 1800s. When Ralph Wilson started the Buffalo team in the American Football League in 1960, he chose Bills after the earlier team and, of course, the mustachioed Western hero.

Why is the No. 42 retired by every MLB team?

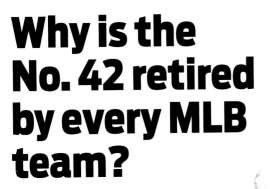

O n April 15, 1947, **JACKIE ROBINSON** became the first Black player in the Major Leagues in the 20th century. Along with being a very talented player, Robinson was a brave person. In the 1940s, many people felt that baseball—and all sports—should remain segregated. After joining the Brooklyn Dodgers, Robinson endured taunts and threats.

Fifty years after Robinson's debut, Major League Baseball retired his No. 42 to honor his courage and his barrier-breaking Hall of Fame career. No Major League players will ever be able to wear that number again. It is officially retired by every team. Each season on April 15, however, every player in the sport wears the number to help us remember the importance of Robinson's life.

Why is a softball called a softball (when it's really pretty hard)?

It could have been worse. Not long after the game was invented in 1887 as "indoor baseball," it was also called mush ball, kitten ball, or lemon ball. (The "ball" in the first game was a rolled-up padded boxing glove!) **THE BALLS IN THE EARLY GAME WERE INDEED MUCH SOFTER THAN TODAY'S**. In 1926, the name softball became official through the YMCA. The ball teams used became harder over time. Today's softballs are 11 inches around and quite hard. A still-soft 16-inch version of the ball is used in a form of softball popular in Chicago.

Why is scoring three goals in a game called a "hat trick"?

The term "hat trick" is best known in hockey, but it's also used in soccer, lacrosse, and other goal-scoring sports. But it started in yet another sport: cricket. In 1858, H.H. Stephenson took consecutive wickets with three bowled balls (that means throwing the ball past the opposing batsmen and knocking over the vertical wooden sticks behind him). Fans at that game were so impressed by the "trick," they took up a collection and bought him a hat.

In hockey, hat trick history started in Chicago. Alex Kaleta of the Chicago Blackhawks had his eye on a hat in a shop, but didn't have enough money with him. The shop owner said if Kaleta scored three goals in a game that night, he could have the hat. After lighting the lamp three times, Kaleta collected his hat!

The tradition stuck, and today, **HOCKEY FANS OFTEN LITTER THE ICE WITH CAPS** after a player scores three goals in a game.

PHOTO CREDITS

Front Cover: Greg Nelson/Sports Illustrated (Giannis Antetokounmpo); Cooper Neill/Associated Press (Patrick Mahomes); Tony Gutierrez/Associated Press (Stephen Curry); Jeff Chevrier/Icon Sportswire via AP (Serena Williams).

Back Cover: AFP via Getty Images (Simone Biles); David E. Klutho/Sports Illustrated (Sidney Crosby); Robert Beck/Sports Illustrated (Mike Trout); NCAA Photos via Getty Images (Jennie Finch).

Associated Press: AP Photo 11 (left), 62, 116; Tannen Maury 10; Kevork Djansezian 12; Ross D. Franklin 13; Schmidt/Pixathlon/SIPA 15 (right); Mark Humphrey 15 (left); Lefteris Pitakaris 16; Paul Shane 17; Michael Alio/Icon Sportswire 25; Nick Potts/PA Wire 34; Kacper Pempel 4 (bottom), 50; David McIntyre/Zuma Wire 56; Ryan Kang 70; Kyodo via AP Images 71 (right); Lai Seng Sin 72; Yomiuri Shimbun 73; John T. Greilick 74; Aaron Favila 79; Al Messerschmidt 84; Icon Sportswire via AP 88; Mark Reis/Cal Sports Media 102; Grigoriy Sisoev/Sputnik 3 (bottom), 108; David Goldman 111; Gray Siegel/CSM via Zuma Wire 113; Amanda Loman 121; David Becker 125.

Getty Images: Bryan Terry/NCAA Photos 59; Laurence Griffiths 5 (bottom), 82; Kyodo News 83.

Sports Illustrated: Robert Beck: 31, 32, 36, 38, 55, 63, 81, 85; John Biever: 52; Simon Bruty: 28, 99; Andy Hayt: 117; Walter Iooss Jr.: 75; Kohjiro Kinno: 91; Heinz Kluetmeier: 18, 19, 43, 64, 80; David E. Klutho: 2 (bottom left), 4 (bottom right), 8, 21, 58, 93, 112; Kevin D. Liles: 54; V.J. Lovero: 77; Bob Martin: 94; John W. McDonough: 2 (center), 2 (right), 3 (right), 4 (top left), 20, 30, 76, 86, 90, 104; Richard Meek: 123; Manny Millan: 63, 68; Donald Miralle: 95; Greg Nelson: 109; Nils Nilsen: 96; Hy Peskin: 78; Erick W. Rasco: 45, 61, 97, 114; Bob Rosato: 25 (right); Carlos M. Saavedra: 98, 100; Jamie Schwaberow: 92; Damian Strohmeyer: 3 (left) 42, 44 (top), 48, 53; Al Tielemans: 11 (right), 24 (right), 39 (left); Rob Tringali: 40; Tony Triolo: 20; Winslow Townson: 39 (right); Fred Vuich: 44 (bottom), 122; John G. Zimmerman: 5 (top), 14, 23.

Others: 123RF: 60 (right), 107 (bottom). Dreamstime: Aspenphotos 110; Lunamarina 115. Library of Congress: 71 (bottom, 2), 122 (bottom). NARA: 51. Shoreline Publishing Group: 107 (top). Shutterstock: Grindstone Photo Group 4 (top right) 33, 46 main; Radu Razvan 35; Ahmad Faizal Yahya 37; ciapix 60 (left); Sirtravealot 106; Joseph Moran 118 (top); Ellie Tuang 118 (bottom); Corepics VOF 119; Chen WS 120; JoeSAPhotos 124.

Acknowledgments

The author would like to thank the diligent and sports-loving staff at Triumph Books for their invaluable help in putting this book together. They are the answer to "what would we do without them?" Thanks to Noah Amstadter and Adam Motin in particular. Thanks to Beth Adelman for her editing assistance as well.